HUNDRED POEMS ABOUT YOU

ROHIT SHUKLA

Girl from the Coast

Contents

Contents

Contents

Contents

Contents

Preface

It's a collection of poems based on love starting from the void and goes stronger with time. Then comes the chaos of love, betrayal, Perseverance, and affinity for some unknown mysterious one that one had never seen,never spoken with.

It's more like a poignant blind love with all the colors of love and notions of life .

We all are just experimenting with love. Till we are young, we keep on falling for others and then there is separation and after that again we fall but we are learning that's why I say love is ritual and is omnipresent. We would never be perfect in it. Throughout our lives we keep learning about it but when it hits us back we feel hurt and the intensity of being hurt would be the same as it was for the first time.

About Author:

Rohit Shukla is an mechanical engineering graduate from a well known Vikram University of Ujjain.

His hobbies include reading intercultural literature and acting. He is a bibliophile and has been an author or co-author of many well praised books. His appetite to learn and an ineffable perception enables him to come up with some amazing heart touching content.

It is said that origin of one's knowledge lies in the perception and rohit's perception towards the world makes him distinguishable.

1. Blindly

Love blindly
Adore blindly
Allure blindly
Trust blindly
Outburst blindly
It's your part play kindly
World is deaf so shout loudly
With stabbing stitches walk proudly
You are over it finally
Again don't be rude behave kindly
And the next love blindly again.

2. Love me

Love me like sun to the moon
Love me like morning to the noon
Love me like planet to the orbits
Love me like batsman to the hits
Love me like clouds to the rain
Love me like the wounds to the pain
Love me like iron to the rust
Love me like tyndall to the dust
Love me like ups to the downs
Love me like heights to the grounds
Love me like winds to the waves
Love me like deeds to the graves
All I need is love to grow again.

3. Love Again

Again I wanna fall in love.
But with whom ?
The one who love me like my mom
The one who scolds me like my paa
The one who can protect me like my eldo
The one who can tease me like a young sibling
The one with whom I can share all my secrets
The one who has answers of all my if's and what's ?
The one who can wait for me like the soil for the first rain
The one who can show me the way like the moon in no moon
day
The one who can wait like a Brook for the ocean paving it's
way
Again I want to fall in love.

4. Virginity

I can dance with a man that won't ask if I'm a virgin or not.
He's my father.
I can walk with a boy who holds my hand to guard me. He won't ask me if I'm a Virgin or not.
He's my brother.
I can talk with a guy till late nights giggling that won't ask me if I'm a Virgin or not ?
He's my best friend.
I can have my head on her lap and watch the sky fully and she too won't ask if I'm a Virgin or not ?
She's my mother .
I know a guy who loves me madly and he doesn't ask if I'm a virgin or not ?
He's my boyfriend.
Then how does someone who doesn't even know me ask if I'm a virgin or not ?

5. Old Banyan And Little Sparrow

You are like the little sparrow

Slapped by the wild winds

And threatened by the raining jets

You just tried to make your childhood dream Of chasing and

surpassing the rainstorm

But it's being said you can't !

Cause you don't have enough what it takes

But you looked the way as few had earlier

So you dared to make it

And you told this all to your favorite banyan tree

That don't have much branches and the leaves as they left him

all

Still he loves the one that comes under him for shelter with all

he has with him.

Now got stuck in the midst of the storm.

It's thundering and you are scared Now the roars make you

more anxious

You was safe under the window visors

But it's hard on you now as you left the safe

Now you can see the same banyan tree ahead but still no

leaves.

How will he keep you safe?

All he is with you this time just trying enough to pluck
himself off the ground for you in this wild winds
With the push of the winds you reached to him.
He hugged you the way he always want to Praising your
courage and hide you
In the sunscald in him.
The sunscald that is filled by you.

6. I'll wait

I'll wait like moon for the sun
I'll wait like child for the fun
I'll wait like oceans for the brooks
I'll wait like stray for the roofs
I'll wait like patients for the doctor
I'll wait like sadness for the laughter
I'll wait like unrests for the rest
I'll wait like sparrow for the nest
I'll wait like butterfly for the bloom
I'll wait like dawn for the noon
I know we are like the two parallel lines
but we will merge at infinity breaking the coordinates
Till then I'll wait♥

7. Autotuned

I was murdering myself

By over thinking

By fears

By guilts

By pain

By anxiety

By unknown doubt's

By misunderstandings

By miscommunication

Then I look for a moment

A Moment in which I can explore my thoughts

The moment where I had loosen myself

The very innocent me

Free from guilts and glitch

I looked my reaction to every little

And asked myself if I'm in the present ?

Or scared by the spooks of past

Or the imminent

Now I'm autotuned.

8. Cosmic You

•

You are like the Cosmos
Always have something unexplored and unexplained
Always unpredictable plenty of riddles
But it's your nature
You have parallel spaces
And so reflected in your persona this fascinates me more
Cause it's all about you
You are somewhere between "To be" or "Not to be"
You are simple imperfect and enjoy your imperfections
Cause they make you more real.

9. Hindrance

In the very next day
I came to know a little more of you
But still it's less
There's a kinda hindrance
That's keeping you safe
And still I'm on my guts
To decode you
I'm like a surfer with board
Breaking the waves toward the shore.

10. Love hurts ?

When we hate it doesn't hurt cause we expect nothing
When we love it hurts cause we expect many things
So what hurts are expectations
It's not love that hurts
Love makes you live.

11. Coastal Love

From your coast
You sent love as showers
I waited season's with ton of hours
I tasted your love in drops
Like the farmers and crops
I kissed you like soil
All the notions are like foils
I want you to notice all my attempts
To read your scribbles like folklores
And the wish to listen you with
All your wishes, fancy fiction and Gossips
For days in hundreds with ton of hours
I will keep you like an ocean to the shells
Closed so independent with own world
But still in ocean being it's part.

12. Restless

Restless days nights with guilts
And sweaty afternoon
That's a symbol that you are
Somewhere in your adulthood
Where you have to wear patience and being pessimistic
Everyday even the last day was your worst
Still keeping the hope
Take your sword
Go for your battle warrior
Just for deeds.

13. Pseudo

I don't pretend
I'm what I'm
I have, what I have
I do, what I want to
I don't like being Pseudo
I don't have grip on words
I know
I'm like a pawn of the board
Still try to castle you in words
But with these baby step
I'll reach your part
To be prompted as super pawn
And can be queen this side
But still in real I'm a pawn
And paving my way.

14. Dark Sides

Let's talk of our dark sides
Till the first star shines
Revealing all our untold secrets, sins, guilts and taboo's
Let's peel our heart layer by layer
To the depth
So in a way we are naked
Naked in our minds
Naked in our souls
We are like two bodies
And a single soul entangled like upper ventricle to the lower
And let's fill all this 4 chambers
With our truths that's free from
These flaws and darkness
Let's wait till the first star
Wave at us with all its strength
And affinity for us
Till then
Let's talk of our dark sides.

15. They Are Here

This monsoon first touches your place

Then it reaches mine

She kissed the air at coast

And infused the clouds with tears of love and notions

They traveled loaded with all your belongings

First the breezes hugs me and kisses me then giving all your love

When asking them about how you are ?

They speak of all your thundering hardships, storming miseries and your echoic screaming nights

Sun of my love reads your letters with me

Thus he knows all about us and start glowing more cause of our love

Instead from peeping the clouds

Showing my glowing love for you

And our love merges this way in spite of our distances

The universe turn this love to a band of colors of life "The rainbow"

The Rainbow of our love with all the patterns of notions as colours

We both can see this from our places

My love you sended love

Sun would say of mine.

16. Logic of love

• 17 •

Love is more like Logic circuit gates
It knows only two input either 0 or 1
0 for null and 1 for 100%
Love follows an "And" operation
It requires both inputs to be 1
To be true and perfect as 1
Be it yours or others part
Or else it's like "Null" having 0
So put your 1 for it.

17. Fragmented Me

I'm just gluing fragmented me

Turning me who was in bits and pieces into a masterpiece all

cause of your fictional love

Even I don't have a clue of you

At noon I thought I'm getting you more

At dawn I'm all clueless

I haven't even seen you

I haven't even listened you

I haven't even talked you

But still

I found you hiding in your words

I found you in the uneasiness of my nights

I found you in my insecurities of you

I found you in your jumbling bubblish words

I found you somewhere in between should or not

Don't know who you are

Even you too don't know

if I'm at your back

For holding at fall

I Don't want any favor from you

All I want is to hear you at 3 in the morning

All I want is to feel you just by side when it's raining

All I want is to sit with you in the park

You on the bench of concrete but your heart to be clay
And I'm on the ground legs folded and listening all your
fictional melo-drama
Your feels, Your thrills
And every single thing
What you hide from the world
You made me do what I always wanted to do
You know what you are the final pull.

18. Fears

Yes I do cry I'm not fake
I too have heart that's pure
I don't love cause I'm insecure
Insecure of the fact that it will hurt
More than it did yesterday
I want to bloom in love
But not be crushed after blooming
I want to make deep dive but I lag in swimming
I think of us to be on the page
It's the lonely sad nights that's like cage
Now it's my heart throbbing today
Don't know why but figuring to find a way
I know tomorrow everything will be set
But currently I'm in unrest
Heart is aching like hell
No memories still I find myself in a well
Perhaps I should stop being a philosopher in love
Cause I don't find myself enough to be loved.

19. One on One

It's always the same
One on one
Wait, what's that ?
I mean always it's you the one
One with devotion whole hearted
That's more like a blind and deaf faith
Faith that never questions
Faith that never Argues
Faith that trust
Faith that believe
Faith that's Pure,and
Faith that can found you in the crowd
Faith that raise over your heart beats
Faith that pushes you
It's in those who walkin
When the rest are leaving
It's in one who never says but there
It's in those who always keep their eyes on you
The one who never let you fall
The one with holds you at fall
The one who knows you are rock bottom
It's always the same one on one
But always like a warrior take you little

Sword and show that at your strongest scream
The one who always there for a call
I don't have contact
I have connections
And I'm at my part as always I was
Now I have to be the brightest star
And I'm self lightened now

20. Love

Love is neither in these 3 magical words "I Love you"
Nor in these 4 magical words " I Love you too "
So where is it ?
Let's look for an honest opinion
It's in the journey
The journey from the encounter to gazing
Form the gazing to the admiration
From admiration to the those pumpkin adores
From the adores to all those words of the first conversation
Conversation now turned to be wired but would always with love
From these conversation it goes to hugs and laughter's
It's in all the scooch's cause of fate
It's in holding and folding at hardships
It's in the celebration of one's day of succes
It's in the 11:11 moments
It's in the 11:59 moments
It's in 3AM calls
It's in pal of silence when night is screaming hard
Basically it's a never ending and blooming journey
From gazing to Stargazing.

21. Gardener

I can't plant a flower
But I can make one bloom
Be this flower is of Lily or my favorite cactus
I want the very sinking flower threatened by wild, thundering
canes to bloom again.
I would put it in light of sun
And water it with love and hopes at dawn
I'm like a Thermal energy reservoir
Like sink I'll absorb all your doubts and fears
And like source I'll make you bloom again
Don't scooch any more because of fate
You found me in heights but I'm not
I want you to have this hand and stand again
Just hold it for once and see now we are at same
Remember this I would always be your greatest audience
Even if you be the last in the race
I'll cheer you being like the first
Because you will lose only in those that are not truly yours
Cause flowers never fails at blooming
This is what a gardener says to every flower.
And too to his favorite cactus.

22. Friendships

Nothing to say

Nothing to prove

It's in those 7 jumbuling of the alphabets

It's a feel and purest and prettiest relation

That's full of innocent bubbles giggles, weird talks, Naughtiest

jokes and sweetest pokes

They always been at your side

At your fall and too on being at top

Even being separated by miles but still

Found themselves in connection everyday and in every way

We been different in our tongue

We been different in our taste

We been different in perspective

But share a common coding of love

And this bind at this age is crucial

Cause it's when you have to look for your belongings

If we can have a copyright of our friendship I would chase to

owe it

Still we are here brought up by universe

With a plan I guess so let's enjoy this bond

And lets lost in the fairy never ending hangovers

That even sourness wouldn't be enough to Dilute the

hangovers

In life we have a choice to be surrounded by people we love
So let's choose the best belongings.

• 26 •

23. Shooting Stars

The people with worst past often
Wear a smile cause they know
How does it feel being there ?
And they won't let other stay on the same page
Cause it's not there choice it's their nature
To make ways like shooting stars
That have limiting life cause
Their heart beat slows down day by day
Cause the universe decided to take all its potential
Even the potential that make their heart beats
Cause they are born as stars
That like a moon itself but with faults like loops
And vacant spaces it's god gifted they can't even complain of
it
Cause it's the plan of the universe.

24. Amidst of thunderstorm

The ship got caught by the high seas
And it's getting tossed by the waves
He is the very sailor with no sign of uneasiness
She gazed him for the control
But still he looks to be filled with same confidence
Now the bow being tossed more than earlier
Like the storm is full of lust
The stern is raised more than earlier
She shouted for him again
But still he reciprocates by asking
How much does she trust him ?
She replied are you out of your mind ?
He smiled and asked the same again
"Wholeheartedly" she said
He replied the same
I trust on the one who puts us here
The one above us all may it be supreme
Or the universe
And have faith in him
Then don't know what worked for them
The winds getting like breeze
The lust turned to love

I guess universe worked cause I readed somewhere
Later that faith can move mountains

• 29 •

25. Northern Lights

I waited years for a glimpse
It's true as the sun is brighter
I would not find you in the sky
Still amidst of these hazy shivering nights
While others planning to have wine and sleep
I got out you look my fate
Many said I'm being foolish
But I dared to believe
As the night is getting darker
I'm shivering and the blood started clotting
I realized that barely can I move my legs
Like they being loaded with tons
I realized my bad
I looked at the sky asking for help
I whispered my dreams to wind
I noticed some windy disturbances in the sky
Even the smallest particle in the universe listening to my
dreams "The dreams of fews".
These smallest particle started working
Then I noticed the sky of my life turning blue and green
Like an ocean upside down Red and pink
Merges for purple
These are those northern lights

The lights that being uncommon
Only few with fortune can have them
But see how lucky we are
Off season still can't stop the universe at its plans
Thanks to these little particles
And these windy best friend always there
At both my lifts and down.

26. Vintage Souls

• 32 •

I'm vintage soul

Not so grown still a toddler

I don't speak

I deal with vibration and frequencies

I don't fall for words

But I can't stop for vibes

I'm only a receiver

I don't make promises

Cause I'm good at commitments

I'm not perfect

Cause I know life is not thermodynamics

I don't have contact

I have connections

With universe

With rain

With coasts

With winds

With little sparrows and chirps

With sunsets

With strays

They gaze at me like the first day

They told me of battling wars of others

They told me of rejections, breaking, separation and sorrows

I don't believe in distances and misunderstandings
I believe in affection
I believe in bonds
Even in hydrogen the weakest bond
So it's a human what we are with
Things will be cumbersome somedays
We need time to fix everything
Still me you and universe
All together here at this time
Universe I'm with you
And you are everywhere
Bring new hopes and believe to achieve what one wants to
Unaffected by any of the upcoming barriers.

27. Dimming Lights

As the light goes dim
I'm on high
All alone looking naked sky
Stars have connection with me since long
They othen guide me
For the tracks that been less brutal
For the hardship that suits my shoulders
I trust them fully cause they been the best partner
Partners of my solace
Patterns of enlightenment
It's the fate again sending me the other way
The way that is less travelled
It's like heck cause it's a different world
Where I can lose a lot
And the chances of the win is minimalist
Don't know how to be calm at this
This is like a migration for me
But like a bliss cause enjoy this work
Hey you stars ?
I want you to again show me my way.

28. All I want

I want you to speak
Speak what ?
Of your boldness
Of your loneliness
Of you spooking past
Of the hardship In craft
Of your personalities
Of your actual individuality
Stay calm take deep breath
I'm not so near but not so far
Although at distance but near at a buzz
I'm not falling for your charm
I'm like a fine arm
I just want you as a Dragonball
One of those 7
Cause one can wish you
And you are different from others
As you are special
Special at trusting
Special at honesty
Special at your crafts
I'm always there
But I won't say

Much cause its not the time
I want you to just slowly surpass this rain
Like a snail
You again be the birds with all your wings
Ready to chase those alarming storms
You are so brave at handling this all
You like supercane
Started making your whirls
At the shore I'm just looking this all
Let's move like the parallel rays side by side
Never trying to merge at a point
Rest we can leave this on universe
It's in universe's hand and ways.

29. Moon's Favorite

I'll meet you at the end of ocean
At the horizon
Where the Suns dips but be star
And the whole night all the stars and
Sun's favorite moon searching her favorite sun
And again from the origin
The sun by stinking
Looking his favorite moon worried
And they both meet for a while
Noticed by only some
Then this greedy world wakes again
Some expecting sun to be there's part
Some expecting moon to be there's
Both have there duties for the day
Still the sun gazes at the moon
And vice versa
The star too claims on moon
But she's the moon that claims Sun
To be only hers
They are so separated but So close
It's natures favorite Love story
And is unconditional
Why are you standing at the coast again ?

Just go It's getting late
You be the moon
I'll you favorite sun
And let's make ours love unconditional.

30. Bright Places

I was there for months
All on my own weeping, screaming, yelling
But so you evaporated from eyes with tears
You are no more in my fears
Then I turned my mood for the bright place
Making my ways by baby foots to the right places
Now can you see where I'm ?
Somewhere in the bright place
I'm not idol
I'm just me.

31. Last Conversation

I remember

She asked for last conversation

But I took that for granted

Now like the rest

She left unsaid

She said she will talk

But

Now she's on journey

Journey of unknown

For which I looked upon the scriptures

To get the pathway

I looked for her steps

As per her last word

She said

She'll never leave me

She wants to live the way

She's born with no guilts and pains

And only with giggling smiling

She's now turned to the shinning star

That guides me at my falls

She often make constellation patterns in the naked sky

She asked the clouds to be her portrait

So that I can still see her glimpse

Her last words
Still remained unheard,unspoken
But we had a language of gazing and vibrations
Still I gaze at her
When the lights at my side are dim
And still she guides me in a way.

32. Every Night

Every night I realize your worth
Every single night of every single day
In every single way
These nights are full of pain and joy
Pain of being parted
And joy of being fortunate to have you at least for a while
Still I find you in the middle of night in very dreams of mine
Still you whisper your mind to get all your if's and what's
Still hear the words of quarrel
The clause of being parted wasn't fair after all
You have you
You also have me
My smile
My way
My thoughts
My dreams
I guess the one that believe in love too
I try to look for you in the every other
But still i don't have you
You are somewhere at the opposite pole
Lost as usual
Clinged more firm to me
I turned the nights dim

And on earplugs dancing like goof
All alone on your favorite song
Until I fell by being exhausted
Every night ends like this
At the verge of the morning
I know I'm far away from you
Still I have you evernight of every single day.

33. Last Wish

I know god
I wished you a lot from you as a child
You have given me what I needed
As per your best perks
But the day when I being told
Not to be toddler cause
Now I'm having the hairs
On my chicks on my chin
My shoulder are getting broader
My voice is getting deeper
I don't fit into my old clothes
Everything changed I accept
My height
My weight
My strength
My thoughts
My minds
Even my faith
But it's my heart
Still childish trusts easily
That beats the same except at times
When I found my vacant space I got
The reason why shouldn't open up

Cause your favourite wishes
Can be stolen by others
That's the saddest part
I wish I could weep badly
So that my throat got choked
After a while my heart
Again started beating
Don't know why ?
It's racing
Then a star crossed by me
I wished this stargazing would last forever
I don't want to hold this
Cause it ruins her entropy
Yes I'm childish and selfish !!
Why shouldn't I ?
Should I be mature ?
Of Course not cause when there is maturity in a relationship
it's get intoxicated
It should be childish
And I love what I love madly !!
I can fall for it
But at least I'm not perfect
That's my best part.

34. Losing Love

It's true I lost her
But inner me says I haven't
She's always with me
If I can write something on her
And it's a book
Imagine of the jumbling minds
And level of understanding
I'm nostalgic
I'm depressed
She only heard you
But it was the me whom she opened her heart
But that only shows
How strong was my love ?
And if it comes to me
I do love her always
I know what love is ?
It's not about
Carrier
Not about faces
Not about distances
It's about those 2 there at time
I only have little words
With her but in minds we talked overnight

I don't have to say much
And she don't have to listen much
All was under this universe
It's the rough time
Low this time and
All I wanted to say
You know how lucky I'm at least ?
I have 2 of your indirect precious plots of me
But it's my call on this
I don't give up easily
Cause I know it's better to give my 100 % to it
And people say its one sided
If it is then also a bliss
That she opened her heart
Being the strongest voice.
In the world of temporary
I'm your forever.

35. Magical Love

She handed love letter
Before leaving
It's in her way especial and magical
With loads of love
She knows me all
But she was my first drive
And would always be
I know how to love her
Unaffected and unconditionally
And I would she was magical
Both in her words and ways
Always messed like me
But never so lost
She's a bliss and bold
She's fearless as lioness
We will merge one day
We been two parallel rays and merge
For sure breaking the rule of coordinates
Again we will go to infinity.

36. Clouds

Each one of us is a cloud
We come in different shapes
We come in different colours
We have different capacities
We have different intensities
Of emotions
Of expressions
Of pain and troubles
Each one of us is a cloud we all have common tears .
Each one of us is a cloud
With a different story
With a different pattern of cry
With a different bullet hole
But a same bandage
Each one of us is a cloud
Someday shiny blue as violets
Some day hazy dark
Each one of us is a cloud
This cloud is gray but not black
Now it's blue
Like his favorite cloud
Cause there were born in pair
Sharing the notions.

37. Clouds And Sun

I know the things are not our ways
But it's on you
We are having tough this time
See whenever you go low
I too go the same cause we are connected
You don't want sun to be low
And I don't want my favorite winds to shattered so
Its been raining here from days or two
But remember I'm with you !!
I know life is brutal at examination
But we have to surpass this all
I'm not sad cause I know
That this will make you sad too.
Have a big hug from your favorite clouds
And then send them to me
I'm there always
See open the window
Put the lights on
And listen your favorite track
We will sure surpass this hampers soon
I'm not rude or angry of you
As I said I'm cool as Ice
You remember the same

Take time
And I'm the same for you
Firmly believe we will surpass this all
Sun always shines
But loves to hide only behind the clouds.

38. Sidewise

Hey peaceful cloud
Can you please
Speak of all your pains ?
Cause of my expectations
And unsaid truths to be told later
Can you please
Bleed all you have on your paper
I know again you got throbbed and hampered
I'm gray somewhat but not dark black
Its easy to comeback like others do
But I won't right now
It will hurt both of us
Cause it's common that randoms do
But I'm not that way
I'll be back soon too soon
Don't worry
I'll be back to you
Like earlier with slow unheard foots
There is nothing like letting you go
And nothing like unnoticed
You are always In my eyes
In my poems
In my dreams tbh

I'm not insecure anymore

I truly believe in the universe

It won't let us down

But time is low at both our parts

Till then we have to be strong

Each single day

Its hard to find sun these days

But you can ask your close clouds

To tell you all

I won't come unless

You want

As I said I'm good at commitments

So I'll be back soon

And I'm not leaving

Cause I don't leave you alone

As always people do

I'm always by your side.

39. Hard Times

Its not only you that is affected
I'm throbbed brutally too
Don't know what's spilling of me
I can't hide this that I'm jolted badly
Bandages and stitches failed to heal this wound
I found myself blue
Under this favorite sky
I too have a guilt of being unnoticed by you
I don't want to be this way
Still I'm at this phase
So consolidated
So broken
I don't know what to call you ?
I don't know what is between you and me ?
Somewhat unclear
I'm not gonna runoff
I'll wait
I'll wait
And then I'll wait
Right from the opening of the eyes
In the 6 to closing shutters at 3 in the morning
I'm Missing your buzz
This is what I felt

I'm not dark black
Still I'm gray.

40. Let's Meet Again

It's within me
It's within you
Let's self ignite
We been born as floret
And blooming in thorns
That's life
Let's work in parallel worlds
I'm glad that I'm also a part
Of your fancy folklores
Be my pain be my bliss
Be my angel
Be my witch
Be my wound
Be my cure
Darling always by your side
With your clouds
And my sun
I don't have any option of giving up
We will meet soon.

41. The Differences

The differences of them and me

I being the silence of night

They being the grunting storms

I being the Chukar bird

They being the Hawks

I don't want to make you mine

I want to be yours

I don't want to see ,how you look ?

I want to read your heart

I don't want all day calls or texts

All I want is a buzz in the morning and night making me good

This way I'm vintage in a say

But I will never strict your flights

In the high skies

I know you won't open your heart to any expect fews.

You told me of

Maybe I'm one of those.

42. Silence

They said it's good to speak.
Speak What ?
Speak of what I have ?
You know what I have with me,Right now ?
Of course not !
I tried to speak of it
But it's unpleasant I guess
Cause that belongs to me
The listener putted on plugs to avoid it
Still I was saying
Then they asked me to move on
But I can't and I won't
Then again they said simply move on.
It's' fine
Nothing new
I won't speak anymore .

43. You are not Alone

You always have a fear
Fear of being appreciated
But being left alone
I'm not leaving you
I'm dark and blue right now
I can't glow cause both
The beats of the heart goes slow
And the mind got numb
Still never giving upon
Your beauty never mattered for me
I got glowed through your words
And still I fear for the day
When you stop writing
You are not alone
You are still in my sight .

44. Go Slow

We are just
Getting the things in its pace
Both never rushed to know the other
Little more or less
Just slowly and sufficiently
The breeze starts blowing
I reached to the coast flowing
Like her favorite cloud
Holding the tip of her forefinger
She too was exploring me
We started understanding the other's pattern
Giving the other butterflies
But then suddenly everything fell to the ground
I know only that
I won't move on because it's not about pretty faces
I got synchronized with her
Don't how but its the fact
Sometimes being slow
Also makes you lose.

45. Poison

I'm like a poison
Start affecting the people
When time being hard to me
I recently done the same
There's no antinode of it
Wise people always read the caution
They move on and many too
Let me there under the same dark place
I have no regrets
Cause I know its my Poison
That effects everyone around
Wise ones know this all
I'm good at being dumb
And only I know how hard these days.

46. Never Give Up

Never give up
Never give up
On the things you love
On the things you do
On the things you are in
On the craft you are working
Sometimes and some days
It's going to grind you hard and harder
But never lose on your drive and decision
Make a move take a pause
Again stand and start over
It will make you for resilient and
Puts a discipline in you
And this way all you have in your hand is constant
improvement
So never give up until you lose
By giving your best.
Then get up again.

47. Come Slowly

Come to me like the clouds
Slowly and silently
Cover me by your love
All your notions
Somewhat blue and heavy with pearls
Let them load your eye lids
Then in drops spill that over me
I'll absorb all your pain
And try to hold you again
Like I do
Come to me by being your
Favorite cloud.

48. Earth and Moon

See how clever this moon is
I was sitting all alone
Under the dark sky
And then i closed my eyes for a while
Thinking of my star
See they started gossiping
The clouds earth's best friend
Making a way trying to bring
Earths favorite to the him
She too was ready to come to her
Favorite earth
And me suddenly looked this
And i smiled at this and winked at the stars
Again i closed my eyes knowingly
Making them love
Cause love only bring love
It never try to break the ones in it.

49. I don't hate You

Its true that a lie can save your heart

But it can break your soul

I can't deny that I loved you

But I would say I don't want you to do the same

I just want to see you blooming

And want to see you developing your wings

To chase the storms and touch your sky

I'm in love with your culture

Your tongue

Your character

Your thoughts

I fell for your words

I haven't pretended anything

I was clear at everything

And I want you to be with me

May be as a acquaintance cause

You make me glow

You set my soul on fire

I want you to speak all your things

And I want you to listen it all like a baby

I won't lie that still I love you

I don't hate you

Standing at the same place.

50. I won't Cry

It's true I won't cry
But that doesn't mean I'm not hurt
Something heavy like tons in weight
It's all upon my heart and mind
The mind trying to calm
But heart is getting failed at breaks
It pumps but induce some emptiness
Don't what but it is
Like dissatisfied like pinching
Like we lost at our best game
I used to talk like a philosopher
But now no more it's like jerk
From the morning to the night
I'm not sad but ultimately
I'm Don't even try to reach out to her
Knowing bleeding again and again
On the paper
Don't know how long this will last
But I don't want to lose you.

51. Commitment

It's like a sense of responsibility

Like a discipline

No one is noticing

Still it's a gesture and kind a perfection

And it's not like mandatory job like promises

But I believe that it's more like punctuality

And one who is good at commitments

Needed not to make promises

And commitment is like putting your best in completing

Be it Work

Be it love

Be it life

Be it friendships

Be it hardships

That's commitment to me

Like fighting for the last inch.

52. Me and the Dogs

They never betray me
When ever i found any dog
I love to say "Hello"
And scooch for some love to them
When I found pups they are
Thick at the middle like a soft pillow
I lift them and play with them
Even mom scolds me to do so
But I can't stop cause
They treat me same even i have rough time
They never judge me
They just came to me with wet kisses
They can't speak but they proves love
And this love is unconditional.

53. Hold On

There would be a time
You would find yourself in chaos
Chaos of rejections
It's hard to get your way
Tons of contact but no connections
Even you can't speak
Time been brutal at checks
All you have is you
Everything loose slowly with passing time
You are like on sand hot at days cold at night
Mind found itself in crossroad
That granny advice to stay away from
You won't be able to trust anyone
Cause you can't anymore on you
But you have to be strong
Like the phenom like a rock
Wear a smile may be fake
But hold on
Cause this will make you firm
And this emptiness will give you solace
Its my experience
They all judge you
Even you scream they pass by

Cause many they see daily so be hard

And they start ignoring but fine

Its ignition of yours

Wait this all will settle soon

Don't lose yourself

You been sectioned

Cause it's hard to give someone hand

Try hard dude don't be rude

Wear a smile still fake but fine

Cause this will give you peace

And being an artist you will get into this role

Try hard but hold on

Try hard but hold on

Try hard but hold on

Try hard but hold on

Still try be rejected And again hold on

In everything, put 100% and

Try for the last inch possibility

And dude hold on.

54. Men and Wolves

Both are same I guess
Cause they share the same pain
They failed at hunts to feed the family
Even being injured try there shot
They try to fix fallings
When everyone sleeping they been on security
They guides the offsprings from experience
They are somewhat loyal like dogs
Even in the shivering cold they been on hunts
They love their belongings and team
They often look lost cause they have insecurities
But bonds of love make them strong
Wolves are not bad but they are mad for their belongings
They always work in team and even chases the death
All at the matters to them is the family
And the leader wolf have the responsibility to set deeds
So we all are like wolf
We care for the old once and guide the youngs
Wolves care for each other as individuals.
They form friendships and nurture their own sick and injured
Like us, wolves form friendships and maintain lifelong bonds
They succeed by cooperating
And they struggle when they're alone.

55. Moon or Stars ?

Young blood with shiny eyes
Dared to loved a shining star
Like one from the bear constellation
So shiny but it's twinkles
Its hidden cause of refractions
Many gaze for it but they passed by
Only a simple boy looked her
Every day adored her with love in eyes
Although it seemed to be at distance of light years
But one wished to see her pattern
He wants her to be in view
They share nights winking the other
Talking in patterns exploring cosmos and the earth
Everything seems well but one day its missed
Cause its the clouds that covers the sight
But now its on one's hand to wait for forget her star
It's a test of patience and perseverance
One should wait for her star to wink again
Clouds will settle some day and
They again wink and talk the same
Hey you listen
"Still I'll choose star over moon"

56. Dear Stranger

Being at opposite poles
I'm here are this north you being at the other
You are stunned and numbed somewhat
You wanna flow like the winds
But it's me the turbulent waves
I was looking for synchronization
To be a tsunami but we failed
You sailed on an unending journey
I'm still somewhat tormed hurting others
And myself
Sorry stranger for everything I did
I wrote these apologies every next day
In hope it will reach you someday or someway
I'm caged now you silence kills me
More than being unnoticed by you.

57. Arundhati and Vasishtha

Will You be my "Arundhati" ?

I will be your "Vasishtha"

You be being my part

We look to the others as one

But we are two

You just try to revolve around me

I'll revolve around you

Breaking the general rule of Cosmos

We been one of the precious stars of the bears pattern

People would like to explore us more

But it's you and me always together

And like in yours tradition

We will gaze and wink to the original someday

I'm shy at saying this

But I have express what I feel

Listen

Can you be my "Arundhati" ?

58. Frozen heart

Although I'm brave
But I have a heart
That have 4 chambers
With 2 upper and lower ventricles
That pumps still have a right to admire
To fell for someone
But now it's freezing
So cold out here
I'm turning to a lame statue
That won't say anything
If striked with a little push
I'll fall down face to ground
This will break that freezing heart
It will stop
And I'm too.

59. Aching Love

To be honest it's hurts as hell
The morning first and the last thought of the night is yours
Everyday my head aches at extreme
I'm lost and getting crack somewhat
This silence kills me everyday
Its like stabbing again and again
I'm wildly and brutally broken
The hopes turned to sorrows
All cause I lose self control
Don't want sympathy
I myself have sympathy on me
For this crawling
I guess now you can understand my words
It's the word in whose mystery
I got stucked
I'm desperately need your patting
I need your words
And if you hate me it's fine !
But I won't hate you
Cause I can't.

60. Darkest hours

I weeped so much that
Eyes waters no more
Even at cuts
Even at bendings
Even at bad health
Even at being broke
But I weeps unconditionally
When it sees the clouds
When winds hit me badly
When it looks all those poetries for you
When it sees the stars twinkling in the sky
Whenever I'm at my deepest and darkest insecurities
I break like hell
I'm broke and will break like glass
When being touched with love
All I miss is you
All I is you
Come back soon
I'm holding on

61. Her first love

Today I'm blessed cause of your clouds
I'm in a strange city with stranger people
All alone trying my best
Walking on unknown streets
Streets with turns like the locomoting snake
Under the blistering sun
I'm walking
Not like walking
I'm heading in some hangover
The sky was all blameless blue
With no seigh of cloud
But after walking some distance of few hundred in metre
I gazed to the naked sky all alone like me for help
Then again after walking few hundred in meters
I found some shadow was traveling over my head
It's like a blowing group of grey clouds
They kinda protecting me from the direct blister of the sun
When I looked at them
I got reminded of you
Clouds being her first love.

62. Trains window

I was sitting to the window of the train
Gazing outside the window
It was months when one of my favourite star left unsaid
All I had now was a single star at the distance of light years
I loved at it as if it was mine earlier
I was gazing it like some madman
It seems as we both had deep acquittance with the other
Then suddenly winds hugged me tightly
This watered my eyes
Now I could see two instead of one
One was the original and the rest
One was mine.

63. Voiceless Volcano

Who me ?
I'm turned to Voiceless volcano
Real Benevolent volcano
Full of anguish of separation
I do have vents that can be seen and felt
I do have foldings and bendings
The tears turned to vapours
That's why I'm hazzy somewhat gloomy
I have been under huge pressure since years
But I have that within me
All I had been told was deceitful truth
All I have now with me is aggression
All I have now is mistrust on the every other
So lost somewhat so founded
The path of truth is stream with obstacles
Don't know what is in my faith
Magma of sorrows is now ready for outburst
All I have with me is tears
The tears in red that are being evaporated
I'm turned to the voiceless volcano.

64. Last Drop

Me being the last drop
Of rain dripping from the last leaf
At the top of the oldest tree
I was falling due to gravity
Or the cause of jolts
Jolts that breaks
Jolts that hurts
Jolts that makes me weep
Jolts cause of memories
Jolts cause of betrayal
Jolts cause of being 100%
If its about perseverance
See I'm like the last drop
Still sticking to the inch of possibility
Do look me for once
I'm still there at the same place.

65. Butterfly

You entered like a butterfly to my life
With all your positivity
You boosted my soul and embraced with love
My lonely soul founded a place of warmth
It gained love and it again started blooming
It somewhat founded its shadow
And It started moving side by side
You being the perfect guide to me
At my falls
Like a single hand of hope
You are somewhat silent
You are somewhat angry
You are somewhat misguided
My love you being the perfect half for me
You know we been mentality connected
I know it's nothing new that someone wishing to you
But all I wished is you
And I would wish is you
You are gone now
But taken somewhat all the negatives
I don't know if you will be back
But I can promise
That their will be no one by side

If it's not you.

66. Nights

It was all ended

Dusk painted sky pink and purple

Now I'm turned to ghost

A ghost with no footprints

I sat up at the darkest ending

Corner of the room

A wedge of moonlight streamed in through the window

I sit in dark everyday,

Knee drawn to my chest

Looking at the stars

Waiting for the night to be over

I remember that day it was hard to rain but

thunder heads rolled in painting the sky Iron gray within minutes

I could see the drops of rain sweeping in and my red tears were sweeping out.

The hissing steady sound of rain was swelling in my ears

Through the blurry rain soaked window of my bedroom

I can imagine her in tears

My eyes were watering.

They call me fool for being in this love

But this is all I have for her

It's my real love for you.

67. Heartaches

When the heart is full of thrills of pain
It feels so heavy
Then only it feels to be more heavier than usual
With all this it aches brutally
Like an heart attack
The eyes turned watery
The ears turned red
The face turned dim ashes
Still with this minor attacks
We do awake in the morning
Awake from your thought
But you are like a never ending hangover
They do not let me sleep and keep me high
I'm terribly walking but still not crawling.

68. I wish

I don't have any wish
Expect at least you know the truth
The truth of being me
The truth of being the one that dares put self secondary
The truth of being honest in every relationship
Be it being a friend
Be it being a brother
Be it being a lover
Be it being a human
The truths that are bold
The truths that are untold
The truths that blisters fully like bright sun
I wish you knew this pain
Of being me .

69. Acceptance

People do scare of my forms
But I'm also a human
I do have notions
I do have heart
I do have tears
I do have pains
I do try to ignore
I do try to adore
I do dare to love
I do have some anger issue
I'm hot as a fire
But cold as a ice too
The door been closed at my face
Still I do dare to knock again
It doesn't mean I'm stupid
It means I'm trying again
Attempts do fail
But I don't give upon anything
Until I tried my best.
Yes I'm a human
I do feel a lot I'm sensitive somewhat
But that's all I'm .

70. First Date

I have plans

That we won't see other

It would be like a blind date

We would meet directly

In some strange city other than our natives

We would meet like strangers

I had a thought that

Our first meeting place would be her favorite place a library

That's full of fictional books with folklores and fictional characters

And amidst of this all we both search for the other eagerly and desperately

We would just try to find the other by peeping through the wooden folders

After innumerable of attempts she would tired

Then an airblow smashed her with an aroma

She was familiar with

It would the same that comes through book of mine favorites that I sent to her

Then she would eagerly following that smell

She would finally reach the chamber where

I would be sitting with a pair of coffee

Blushed turned her cheeks red

She would have nothing to say
All she would try to peep through the book to see me.

71. A poem

It's the way we bleed our draining
Notions in to the paper
The very life less paper
We add colors to it as
Our notions to the life
And we are the artist of this poem
So let's do it
Perfectly with all the true color of joy and happiness
The colors of life and love
At least I do write what I feel
I turn pain to poetries.

72. Social Misfits

I'm a social misfit
Cause I'm somewhat vintage in thoughts
Cause I do choose forgiveness over revenge
Cause its hard for me to lie
Cause I do trust blind
Cause I don't betray
Cause I dare to talk the strangers
Cause I dare to help the one in need
Cause I don't use anyone's kindness
Cause I do care for what I love
Cause I dare to take my stands
Cause I dare to be the same at face and at its back
Cause I don't have double standards
Cause I dare to be bold at words and action
Cause I love and cares for closers extremely
Cause I'm emotionally sensitive as hell
And sometimes rowdy at peak.
Yes I'm a social misfit.

73. Eclipse

We are parted like eclipse
It's not our fault
It's the else that been between us
We are so separated but so close
Its for a while but we will again be on others gaze
Lets surpass this time
With perseverance and efforts
Soon these vapors of uncertainties will settle down.
We will soon be the same .

74. Imperfect Relationships

There is nothing like perfect relationship

All we need is a person

That can make our heart bloom

That can set your soul on fire

That can enjoy your weirdness

That can enjoy spending time with you

That can scream of your silence

That can sense the wetness of your kerchief

That respect your dreams

That can bear your screams

That can give you hugs at falls

That can scooch down to make full tall

All I want the one that always chooses

Neither me nor you

But "us"

If you find anyone so

Please don't lose the one

Cause it's love

And it's imperfectly perfect.

75. What I Need ?

Please warm me with your hugs
When the things are cold between us
Endure me in love
When the things are rough between us
Glue me with trust
When everything is falling between us
Pour me more and more with love
When there is drought of feelings we share
Please start the conversation first
When I don't talk you first
Please hold me tight
When I try to make the distance
Please listen to my screams
When I pretend to be calm.

76. Second Chance

It's nothing new
If I had been misunderstood
I don't blame anyone for anything
Its my make that I lose that's close to me
I had loosen many things and people
And if I think of my role
I found some mistakes
But that doesn't proves that
I ain't deserve a second chance
Ask yourself
Ain't I ?

77. River and Shore ?

Can you be the river ?

I'll be your shore

I know there's a fraction of possibilities

But I believe in universe

And who knows till when we have our breaths?

All we have now in hand

We can be together forever in now

But I'll still love you like the shore

I'll love you like the shore

With every waves of notion in you

All I found is a way of you

I'll stay the same as I was.

Can I ask you again?

Can you be river ?

I promise

I'll be your shore.

78. Dreams or Disaster?

Life is always a mesh
I'm turned on it like 6
But all I'm is 9 out of 10
I do have fear
And I too have a dream
Dream that is much of others than being mine
I do need a control on
Passion and profession
Some days I'm High
Some Days I do fall
So hundreds of kilometers from home
All strangers none of my own
People with different tongue and taste
I do feel like a cage
Its like adversity
But still being the bravest character
I don't know if
It's dream or disaster ?

79. Can I take you ?

Can I take you ?
To my Fictionland
Where we can inhale and exhale
The dreaming Folklores
Can I take you ?
To yours favorite writers place
Where you can have answers
To all your if's and what's
Can I take you ?
To your favourite place
Of Worship
Where you always loves
To pray
Can I take you ?
To the place so Heighted
That you can see
Heights of truth and lies
Can I take you ?
To the place where
All yours trouble
Would be mine
Can I take you ?
To the place

Where there no scarcity
For anything
Everyone have just sufficient
Can I take you?
To the place
Where there are standards of love
Which we read in Books
Which we love to be in
Can I take you ?

80. Me

I do sound matured
But I'm like a small kid only
That's weeps at falling
That searches for warmth
The hardest and heaviest fear for me
Is my health
When I fall on it I break like hell
I been turned to fragments
I want someone
To have my hand pull me up
Saying I would be alright
I would be the same
In strength
In thoughts
In everything.

81. Long walks

It's get dark so early nowadays
Would you like to go for a walk with me ?
We will again walk like our first meet
You again feel awkward to speak first
Again I'll be the one to start the conversation
Again I'll start like a dumb about the whether
Again you try to hide the blushing giggle on my stupidity.
Again I'll try to ask you to walk by the side of the footpath.
Again I'll walk to the side where the vehicles are passing.
Again we will move to the ending corner of the street.
Again we will be in unrest of getting noticed
Again we try to break the silence between us by the strokes of
shoes.
Again at the end of the corner you wait for the hug.
Again you try to mark something on the ground waiting for
the first hug with your head down.
Again I'll be the one to make you close
With this we will start something again.

82. Just hold my hand

At your every fall
I'll hold you like a snowball
At your every emotional unrest
I'll endure you for the best
At your every black out
I'll be the one that safe you out
When you being runner up
I'll cheer for you like you holding cup
When you get low
I'll giving you a kissing air blow
When you feel burn out
I'll ask you for your favourite check out
When you fell for stars
I'll lullaby on strings of guitar
When you scooch cause of tides
I'll take you to the rides
Darling I'll hold you like a child
I'll give you moon and sun at your bedside.

83. People's choice

He who waits to stop for you to join

He who loves to tie your shoes.

He who shift closer to you when you're subconsciously moving away while you're walking next to him

He who can listen to your screaming silence

He who decodes your codes.

He who smiles at you as soon as you make eye contact.

He who seeks you out to tell you some good news.

He who listens to you and hears you and understands you.

He who is making efforts instead of the If"s and what's

Do not make the mistake of ever convincing yourself that everyone is bad

Just think how he's doing this all fighting against all odds daily.

84. Leaving

If you really want to leave
Don't leave please
Still if you have to then also
Don't leave please
I can't afford that
I want you tell me everything about you that you never said
to anyone
I'm like your shadow
Please let me know of your darkest and the brightest secret
Tell me of the person that you admire the most
Tell me of the person of the fate your first love
Tell me all about you
I'm eager to know
Still If you want to leave
Please don't leave
Be always in my gaze and have mine at times
I'm the most cursed unloved one
Who thought of being loved by someone
And say what you honestly think of me
Being the cursed
I'm okay but
Please don't leave me .

85. Death Bed

If I died today
Don't tie my body to the stretcher
Cause I love to be free
Don't put much fragrance over me
Cause i love to be simple
Don't cry much for me
Cause you know
I hate to see others in tears
Don't try to hold me long on stretcher
Cause I don't like to be burden
Burn me at place where there's a riverine nearby
Cause I love ghats
Burn me at a open area
Cause i hate being caged
Don't leave me alone
Till my body get burned fully
Cause I hate being alone at burned out
Take out all my writing works
And especially letters for love
Send it to them
Saying all my love for her
Don't tell her that
I'm no more

Every next day ask her
How she's ?
Even she replies or not
Don't be arrogant
Even being ignored
Just don't let her alone
Don't spend too much on my funeral
Make it as simple as I'm
Earning less sleeping with peace
Invite everyone for the funeral
Ask them to confess every single truth
And every single lie of mine
Tell everyone how everyday and every time
How I cured myself ?
Standing against all odds
Dreaming and daring to work for
Tell everyone about all my wars and victories
Even of failures
And the foremost
Please be the one to share one's pain
Be it an stranger in need
Then slowly I'll turned to corpse
Reduced from kilograms to grams
Then take me to the holy place
Of Kashi at the feet of the supreme
Where Always I dreamt to be
And mixed me to the water

With reciting my favorite verses of mine
So that I can be loved by waves
This way I'll sing.

86. Unloved ones

We all are the unloved ones
In search of our beloved ones
We been traveling since long solely
At the end ending truth we are lonely
I too still proud on me being me
Cause I know how I many sobers glee
I traveled like an barefoot immortal ghost
With no foot marks wandering the Coast
All I was trying to find a house
That gives me warmth,comfort,love
But then someone touched me behind
Another wandering unloved one all I found .

87. Confession

I'm simple but always dark in life
Even I don't have favorite colors
I try my best shot at everything
But I do need confessions
I'm mad at you
Don't know why I do say
I'm cause of ways
You want me, say it then
I'm dying for thousand years
I have none like you
Many gaze at me
when they look in the eye
All they find is you
So please do confess
In your codes
I'll decode them
Read it for thousand time
Like an addict
Do confess
How mad are you for me?
How do you hate yourself for loving me ?
How you can't stop yourself from falling ?
How badly do you want me ?

88. Can you wait ?

I'm ready to fight
With the world
I don't know of people
But I promise
I won't change
I'll love you with same intensity
I'll listen to all your write-ups
Even you turned to your 60's
I won't go for carrier,your looks,your language
You are born so
I don't want to change a thing
Still being the paradox
I'll keep you as first daughter of the family
I'm ready for every rifts
I'm ready to work on my goals
But you promise you will wait
You will have your eyes over the horizon
At the end of the ocean
You will wait in my hope
You will ask the clouds,sun,moon,
Even the winds to care of me
I'll be tsunami for others
But end like a slow wave

At your waiting foot
On the shore
You please wait
I'll come sure
I'll take all your pain
Till then to love me
I need your love and hand
Cause only you guides me
Gives me strength
Can you wait?

89. Universe

Love me the you want to
I have no complaints
All i have is smile
That i was loved
I don't know where you are
I don't know how you look
But when I see clouds
They form a shape of yours
Little gloomy
Little clear as crystal
Sometimes like the fog
Sometimes as blistering sun
All I have a mute and cute
Little folklore of us
Yes it was never you or me
It's us always
And always it will be us .
Lets wish together
For the other to be on the others fate
I'm in rush
I'll wait
And let's see
what's in the universe's womb.

90. Sufficient You

What do you want ?
Just sufficient you
Who can stop my racing heart
Who can stop me at explanations
What do you want?
Just your soul
Not you not me
All i want is us

What do you want ?
No confusion no confusion
Only gazing and gesture
And Little care and dare
What do you want ?
You to hold my hand
You to share our plans
You to be hand from nowhere
What do you want ?
A butterfly
With all its natural effect
Wandering the way she wants
But back to her favorite flower.

91. Distances

Not only separate us
But also our common paths
We miss others gaze
We are so far still so close
I don't have a clue
If I'm coming close
Or I'm getting farther
But one day there would be a
Bridge of love between your hearts
Parting the distances.

92. Why not me ?

It's not about few memories

It's about all the thrills and goosebumps

It's about the amazingly experience

Of being together still separated

I was hurted i won't lie but I don't mind it

I know its hard for you everyday

It's not easy being you

I know you are perfect in every role

Being a daughter,Friend, Profession, and a lover too

You are special in every way

For me i meeted you by the fate

But i love the fact that i meeted you

I Haven't seen you but it never mattered to me And never would be

I found you perfect in everything

You open our heart for a while but

I still remember each and everything

You was my favorite

You are my favorite

You would always Be

It's not about looks or taste

It's about us

I don't want to lose a connection with you

Till i have my last breath.

I know we have seperate dreams

We Need focus but still we need love

Care, Pampering, a hand from nowhere at falls I'm imperfect

You being the star for me

Always just try to a have a second thought

I want you to be top of everything you do

We are vintage see being in new age

We paas Letters

When I have your new letter

My lower ventricle filled

With fluid or i guess its the blood that chases

The valve to run out

You know what you are to me

I find you blooming in the drops of the unopened water tap

I find you somewhere in the partition of noon and dawn so coloured

I find you in the chirps of the sparrow to the hooting of the owl.

I find you somewhere in the nocturnal chorus in the night .

I find you in the diverse nature my love

So I won't mention you in the old metaphors.

93. Diary

Take me out of your bookshelf
I don't want to die in the pages of your dairy
I missed your letter quite often
So this time too
I'm suffocating in the caged A5 sized space
I feel much comfortable in your 4 chambered place
I love to rush in the matrix of your blood with hormones
Giving you all the peace
And space excluding this cruel world
Although I hate being caged
But I love the way you put me in words Its euphoric to me
I'm Always in long lasting hangovers
I want you to take me out of your bookshelf.
I'm lazy and missed your letter again.

94. Chaos and conflicts

We all waste our time in conflicts and chaos
Instead of blooming together
Enjoying every precious second
We often been unsure of the future
Than being there at instant
We often look for the possibilities
Than striving it madly
Me being personally have the same heart
That weight around 300gm
Pumps the same mixture
But it races more when got feared
It aches like roots are being plucked off the ground
Do you know why it happens ?
I'm also human i weep
Why do you fear to say it ?
Why do you fear to respond ?
Say if you find me another star
Pretending to be your moon ?
You can love the moon being
At farthest from you
And me being at distance you few words
Deserve nothing except being unloved
Being the voiceless scream .

95. Secret Admiration

Break me with your silence

Fix me with your words

Love me secretly

And say it silently

How long will you let your mind

Control your heart ?

How long will you

Keep fooling your neurons

Blocking their path ?

How can you fade all my memories

About sneaking to your room while you sleep ? How can you

hide your tears of happiness When you felt you loved me ?

How can you hide the wounds

That hurted you cause of me ?

How can you face the rain of the Coast

That had my smell every time ?

How long will you erase my name from

The last page of your every notebook ?

How long will cut the names of us

You are calculating our love percentage ?

Why do you always complain about me ?

96. Kite Runner

I'm drowning more in love
The distance thousands in kilometers
And journey of unending days and nights
It's like flying kites high in the skyline
Trying to pull you back with every jolt
But the wild winds turned you upside down
You are keep rotating
Clock and anticlock
Dragged closer and farther to me
I'm trying to you hold you with peace
With all your good and swings of mood
We are connected with a string
You was just rising high in your limitless sky
And me being child cheering your flight
But all upon sudden
It's the winds that hampering and hammering Us now
I try to pull you closer slowly
I fear what if the wind will rule me?
What if the wind rules me?

97. You

You know you are reason
You cure me everyday
Your smile bring a smile to me
Your teasing and pullings just sufficient to me
The way you scold like grandma
The way you cares like maa
The way you just boomerang with words
The way you stitches the Withereds
You know what innocently you do everyday?
You sow a seed of hope and love
Which is enough and a good cause
You just !
Don't know how to express
I'm not poetic don't even look like
But still I'll say
You just hide your bruises and wounds
Trying to smile each day
But I know of your battles
I'm here for your scars,scalds,bruises and deepest wounds
I'm here in the corner of your room
I'll clap when you will try
When no one knows your efforts
I'll be the audience don't worry

Being your sun I'll pull you up in the darkest days
See
Just I'm smiling and thanking the universe
To have you at my part.

98. Me before You

There's nothing like "me before you" in love.

As if the people say put yourself first.

I found it a lame excuse to hide your cowardness to fall for someone

If you truly love someone or ever had,

You better know it's gonna be "You before me"

Whatever be the thing if its good its gonna be like "You before me "

And when its something pity it would be "Me before you"

I find it as a mere excuse

Cause if you're in love

You can't control your heart

Your mind will try to but notions gonna overrule the thing.

So if you think you would have a balance then

Please ask yourself, Is this love ?

No right ?

And then comes a second thing self love

Self love it can give you some peace

But if you find your peace in your love

What to do then ?

It's complicated right

Now someone will say nothing like love exists. Is it so ?

No again cause if it's not so we are not here hearing and
reading the great mighty classical love stories.
And now you ask yourself
Is this true or not ?
We often feel it for someone
May be we meet him/her or not
May be we have seen or not
But still there's something that give us a peace
It's not attraction or affection
It's something unending and unexpressed
Just the puts us all on cloud nine
We wander like a butterfly
And it's
Just unexplainable
Love can cling our hearts
But it liberates our souls .

99. Him and Her

He's sun but still affected by the eclipse
He loves his moon since years
Unaffected and unconditionally
With no logics only with magic
In Spite of the distance
He gaze at her with love
She knows this all
They both fear of love
He knows all of her fears and insecurities
That's why he never says openly
About his love
He knows of all her secret admiration for him
Although she says of herself to be meshed
But then he says if his messy hairs
They both laugh at his weird thoughts
Their love is visible in their eyes
They both are vintage in the world of modern love
They both still believe in the fundamentals of love
When he read her in her bleedings and outbursts
He turned to tears due to her love for him
Cause had never ever been loved so
Now he knows how much she loves her
This is the love that the universe preserved for him

He just feel the concern as from mother for him
Sometimes he got stuck in the glitch of fate
But he was in war since long with a batch of bravery
They both pretend to be carefree but always missing the other
She loves to scold him and tease him
Noticing all his attempts to say his heart
She loves the way he tries to convince her
when she pretends to be mad of him
He too know of all her secret admiration
It's unique they both know this
In spite all the differences and distances in them
They share same habits like weeping and loving
They are together all under the sky using clouds as messengers
And the sun and moon being the other half of them
They exchange their sun and moon sharing their love
Although he had never seen her but he can identify her in
billions
He knows she sometimes got shivered in the nights cause of
the brutal past
So he always keep his eyes on her
He just hold her hand and presses it with love
Then she blushed at this care
Both saying the other to be perfect
They enjoy their imperfections
They fight, they love, they laugh, they live
They just end with their forehead touching others
And both in tears saying all about their missing for the other

He's imperfect and different from others.
Sometimes he falls by fate this time too.
He's not going anywhere, always with you

• 127 •

100. Destinations

Why can't we make things up to destination ?

In this journey it's sure we will reach somewhere someday.

So why not strive for a common place ?

You come from your path

I'll from mine

Working and worshiping for our wisdom

We won't say anything to anyone

This would be between all you and all me

Cause I dream of the day with sunrise and sunset set with you

And whatever way your are, just trust

Say it at least

You better know I can't say

Cause you better know what I fear the most about you

In Spite of all pattern, behaviors, differences

We can try to be the best I know its hard but still

I'm not into reels,I'm into reality

It's not about pretty faces or smile

If I have millions still I'll choose you

Cause I believe in a saying of mine

Don't love millions

Just love one in million ways

Love is an abstract entity which cannot be explained in words, we learn about by our experience and we continue to get an outlook for it. But after a while we come up with our own explanation. But whenever we realize it, it brings calmness, completeness and internal satisfaction of having something. Something that is more than enough. Just something extra like having more ice cream than your sibling. This extra thing brings you a confidence that even if you will loose still you will have something that can never be taken back. Love is something which is surplus.

The one who has this ineffable and indescribable experience are the lucky one.

But not everybody is fortunate enough.

What do you call love?

Is it a result of excessive imbalanced hormones, which will go away with age or is it something else?

You will have to find the answer yourself and there is no wrong answer to this question.